MIKE & MARGARETH'S NO-NONSENSE GUIDE FOR COUPLES

How to Manage Conflict, Communication & Compromise in Your Relationship

MICHAEL SANDS & MARGARETH GARNIER

ACKNOWLEDGMENTS

We are grateful to Andy Mendelson for his creative input in helping us shape this book. We thank Jennifer Hickman and Daisy Simon for their feedback and help with copy editing.

Others who read the manuscript and gave valuable feedback include Sigena Sugar, Robin Sands, Joelle Valme, David Pine, and Alex Simon.

We salute partners who have had the courage to examine their relationship through the therapy process and commit to act in a more caring and respectful way toward each other.

TABLE OF CONTENTS

MIKE'S INTRODUCTION

In over 20 years as a psychotherapist in private practice, I never seriously contemplated writing about the ways that I have helped couples improve their relationships. Looking back, I suspect the reason is that in my personal relationships I had not been able to live up to the methods and techniques I used so effectively with couples. For some miraculous hard-to-pin down reason, my relationship with Margareth has enabled me to use all my experience, skills, and pain to build a deeper, caring relationship with her. This is not to say that our relationship has just been all warm and fuzzy but that we've been able to manage the difficulties, disagreements and discord (our respective baggage, basically) in a way that has helped us grow as individuals and as a couple.

As our relationship lengthened, Margareth suggested that people might benefit from reading about how I have helped couples mediate their differences. I was initially resistant, feeling that the cognitive-behavioral work I did with couples didn't lend itself to this form, that most of what I did was based on communication guidelines and techniques that have been mostly written about and used over the years by couples therapists. So I wondered whether anything significantly new would be added to the massive amount of literature on relationships. Margareth begged to differ, believing that there would be something of value in combining my direct, highly active style with couples, especially in a shorter more concise form, with her experiences in long-term relationships and her work as a judge and mediator. So Margareth and I embarked on this journey together and we are happy to share the fruit of our labor with you.

I wanted to use these introductory remarks to explain the nature of my work with couples who want to stay together but are having a hard time making it work. One observation that has consistently stood up over the years is that – no matter a couple's socio-economic status or ethnicity or cultural background – ANY problem in a relationship can be resolved as long as the parties are truly committed to each other, and NO problem can ever be resolved if the parties talk to each other in a hurtful, disrespectful, or aggressive way. The desire to help facilitate communication that is caring, even when there is conflict, has been the main focus in my work with couples. As my practice evolved, I began to establish clear-cut communication rules for couples who were, for the most part, happy to subscribe to a system that could help reduce the disorder in their interaction.

However, I found that even when partners agreed with the wisdom of these rules and applied them during arguments, the change did not last very long. The emotional temperature in an argument was such that one partner telling the other that a rule was being broken and expecting his behavior to change right then and there was like throwing a pebble into the ocean and expecting it to make an appreciable impact.

I realized that in order to help clients change their communication habits, I had to find ways to stop toxic interactions at the exact moment they were occurring. To help exercise restraint in these moments I established code words that couples would use when certain rules were being broken or when one partner was on the verge of breaking one. The utterance of a code word would stop all verbal communication between partners followed by a period of physical separation.

While this initially appeared reminiscent of the time-outs given to children, it proved effective in limiting the damage caused by hurtful exchanges. When partners used a code word, it produced an odd kind of teamwork, a feeling of "we're-in-this together," and a sense of power over their tendency to derail the partnership by communicating destructively. Partners often realized that if they had to use something as "silly" as a code word, then their relationship was really in trouble and much more care was needed to improve the way they talked to each other.

I could help couples talk more constructively, I could give them techniques that would help them exercise restraint in critical moments, but this was still insufficient to help couples fully resolve their differences. The key factor resided in their ability to compromise, to accept less than what was ideally wanted with the knowledge that compromise would better serve the relationship.

Unfortunately, the beliefs each partner brought to the relationship often interfered with the couple's ability to compromise – beliefs that may have come from the culture, peers, or family background. These beliefs occasionally led partners to want me, the therapist, to declare that one's partner's need was more appropriate or more normal than the other's. Short of situations where there was substance abuse or risk to one partner's safety, I have tried to help couples realize that their needs are simply different, with no one's need being superior. Over the years, it's been gratifying to see that for couples who learn how to compromise, virtually any problem could be resolved no matter how complex or what area covered.

The case examples in this book are composites and do not represent any particular individual or couple that I have worked with. The use of the masculine pronoun is simply for grammatical convenience. While this book seems to have been written for heterosexual couples, the principles and techniques apply to relationships of any kind in which partners are truly committed to each other.

MARGARETH'S INTRODUCTION

I had it all wrong through the years! Not taking my ghosts into consideration, I kept tying the knots with partners full of identical or bigger ghosts. I felt sorry for myself, feeling constantly tired of being alone amidst relationships.

Three successful sons and three grand kids later, I decided to follow my friend's advice supported by my last son's constant reminder that time is of the essence. I turned to OK Cupid to find a partner.

I got lucky.

I found someone who was conscious of and ready to expose his ghosts, someone who, like me, was looking for that last relationship.

I was never promised a rose garden. Every time my old habits surfaced he addressed them in a way that did not leave me feeling panic and when his issues showed their ugly heads, he acknowledged them without false pretense. In time, I was able to see that there was a pattern in Mike's responses and interaction when we were at odds with each other. Through the crucible of our discord, we decided to try the methods and rules of communication that he used on couples. Over time, with the inevitable push and pull of our various needs, it worked. I became so excited that I didn't want to keep it just to myself. I recommended that we write a book together to help other couples simplify their lives as mine was simplified, thus this swell book.

Enjoy!

CHAPTER 1

THE 24-HOUR RULE

© Mike Baldwin / Cornered

"Look, I said I was sorry five years ago.
Quit dredging up the past."

PREMISE

It is natural in a relationship of any depth to harbor resentments and grudges. Reflecting on old wounds – how they connect to our past, why we continue to have to deal with them in the present – is important for our personal growth and deserves attention. However, arguing about things rooted in the past rarely produces greater closeness between partners. Therefore, issues need to be brought up as soon as they occur and while fresh in our minds. If we hold things in, we tend to express them inappropriately, often explosively. And the damage from such communication lasts well beyond the time of its expression.

HOW THIS RULE WORKS

All grievances must be discussed with your partner within 24 hours. If for any reason you fail to discuss a grievance within 24 hours of its occurrence, you lose the right to bring it up. Forever! Period! End of story! Here is what you do:

1. Establish a code word with your partner that will be uttered when a grievance falls outside the 24-hour window. The code word you establish must not be critical of your partner or his behavior. So, code words like "again" or "idiot" would

be unacceptable. For this rule, I will use the word "asparagus" but feel free to choose your own.

2. When that code word is uttered, conversation stops for 15 minutes AND you must get out of each other's line of vision for that time period.

3. During those 15 minutes, do something that is calming – breathe deeply, listen to music, read a book. You do not have to dwell on the recent interaction with your partner if that continues to make you feel tense.

4. When the fifteen minute break is up, you may resume contact with your partner and continue the conversation (you don't have to) as long as this rule is being observed.

Once the code word has been uttered, you may not debate whether the code word was used appropriately, attempt to explain why it was necessary to bring up the past, or follow your partner into another room as he attempts to effect a 15-minute separation.

Common Objection to this Rule: "Why shouldn't I be able to bring up the past since it happens over and over again?" If that's the case, no need to reference the past since the behavior is certain to recur in the present, at which time you will have the opportunity to bring it up within 24 hours. As tempting as it might be to bring up the past and shame your partner into changing his behavior, it just does not work over the long term. And worse, it sets up a precedent on how to address the other's behavior when one partner is dissatisfied.

WHY ARE YOU BRINGING UP THE PAST WITH YOUR PARTNER?

Try to understand why you are having trouble letting go of the past. This knowledge can help you figure out how to deal more effectively with your partner's current behavior and your reaction to it.

Grievances are often not brought up in a timely manner because of fear: fear that your partner may become angry or defensive; fear that if he ignores you, it may make you feel uncared for; fear that his indifference may trigger your anger and cause you to act badly. Also, you may fear making matters worse if you don't know how to bring up something in a constructive way.

HOW TO ADDRESS YOUR PARTNER'S BEHAVIOR

In the 1950's TV show, *Dragnet,* Sgt. Friday coined the phrase, "Just the facts, ma'am," to prompt people to tell him only what they saw and heard. The same approach should be used when first addressing your partner about behavior that is upsetting to you. Be as specific as possible about what occurred and when. If you can't cite chapter and verse, hold your tongue until you can. In addition:

Speak as you would normally. If you can't, it's better to wait before talking to your partner.

Avoid words like always, never, should, have to, or must.

Do not psychoanalyze what childhood or other historical factors may have led your partner to act a certain way.

Do not bring something up if you are feeling hot under the collar. Wait until you feel less compelled to communicate with your partner.

Do not bring up anything first thing in the morning or late at night or after alcohol (or any other substance) has been consumed.

Do not raise emotionally charged issues by text, email or phone or in the presence of a third party.

CHAPTER 2

NO FINGER-POINTING,
PLEASE

"Our relationship would be
perfect if it wasn't for you!"

PREMISE

You cannot treat your partner as an object who is displeasing you and expect that partner to care about how you feel. If you attack or blame, the response will invariably be aggressive, defensive or withdrawing. However, when you speak from your own needs and feelings, it gives your partner the leeway to care about you.

HOW TO EXPRESS NEEDS WITHOUT BLAMING YOUR PARTNER

Of all the rules in this book, this is the one that couples have the most difficulty with. A partner's anger often finds its expression in blaming the other. The clearest indication of a blaming statement is one that usually begins with the word "you," as in "You never listen to me" or "You're never there when I need you." Needs should be expressed in the following ways:

1. **Description of the behavior (or non-behavior) that makes you unhappy.**

   The behavior must be as specific and observable as possible in order to give your partner the opportunity to effectively respond to your need. The desire to feel more loved or cared for is certainly an understandable emotion, but it is too

vague for a partner to satisfy. It is your responsibility to figure out what behaviors you can ask
of your partner that would make you feel more
appreciated. Examples of specific behaviors
include things like wanting to hold hands in public, needing more foreplay before sex, wanting to
share your daily work experience, or discussing
discretionary purchases before they occur.

2. **How the behavior made you feel or the tangible effect of the behavior**
This involves sharing your feelings with your
partner. Just asking for behavioral change without helping your partner see the emotional impact
makes it less likely that you will get the desired
result. Let's suppose you are dissatisfied because
your partner rarely shares what went on during
his workday when he comes home. It might be
helpful to tell him that knowing so little about
his workday makes you feel less close and less
involved in his life.

3. **What Specific Behavioral Change You Expect**
To encourage your partner to be responsive to
your needs, you will need to be as specific as
possible about what your expectations are. In
the case of wanting him to share more of his day
with you, you might suggest that after he comes

home from work and settles in, both of you talk about each other's day for ten minutes. Or if you want your partner to help with the housework, you might suggest a specific task at a specific frequency. Partners experience relief when it is clear what the expectations are (even if they can't totally fulfill them, as is usually the case).

It is important to keep in mind that you cannot convince someone to feel a certain way towards you. Legislating emotions just doesn't work. However, while emotions are out of your immediate control, you have total power over how you choose to react to them and how you communicate them to your partner.

EXAMPLE OF HOW TO EXPRESS YOUR NEEDS TO YOUR PARTNER

Correct Way: When you get up and leave your dishes on the table, I feel irritated with you. Since I've already prepared and cooked the meal, I don't think I should have to wash the dishes too. It feels overwhelming! I would like you to wipe down the table, throw the scraps in the garbage, put the dishes in the dishwasher, and I'll take it from there.

Wrong Way: You're a slob, you're always leaving your dirty dishes in the sink and I'm sick and tired of cleaning up your messes.

The above should not be seen as a semantic manipulation; it is not simply about putting "I feel" in front of every critical thing you say. "I feel you're a pig…" is, in essence, no different than saying "You are a pig." This rule is about changing how you talk to your partner, stepping away from accusing to expressing your needs and feelings.

Code Word to Use When the Rule Is Being Broken

Just as in the first rule, the code word you established with your partner should be uttered when either of you is blaming the other. All conversation would immediately stop, and you would remain out of each other's line of vision for 15 minutes. If you are in a car, an admittedly more difficult situation, you might turn your head away from your partner (as long as you're not the driver, of course) or, if possible, pull off the road.

Code Word to Use When the Rule Is About to Be Broken

We all know when our emotional temperature is rising during an argument, when we are getting close to losing it. At that point, in order to avoid damaging the relationship, it is imperative that all conversation stop, even though NO rule is being violated. To do this, you and your partner would establish a new code word to be used when either of you is on the verge of violating this rule. To continue my attachment to vegetables, I often suggest "broccoli" as a new code word (but, again, feel free to choose your own).

Uttering this new code word would tell your partner the following: Out of respect for our relationship, and the agreement we made to observe this rule, it is better if we take a break for now. I realize that I'm not able to speak constructively and I'm getting to the point of losing it. Once the code word is uttered, all conversation stops and you separate for 15 minutes.

WHAT MAKES BLAMING SO IRRESISTIBLE?

In order to break the habit of blaming your partner for your unhappiness, it is important to understand the reasons for this behavior and what you might be getting out of it. The reasons often involve:

Feeling Like A Victim: When feeling relatively powerless, we tend to resent the person who is "making" us feel this way. As a result, we often try to overcome this feeling by acting aggressively or explosively, especially if the behavior has been going on for a while.

Modeling Parental Behavior: We often perpetuate our parents' behaviors, and it may pose a problem when their dialogue was filled with statements like: "you are this" and "you are that."

Impulse Control: With friends or on the job, our impulses seem fairly controllable. In intimate relationships, impulses often get the better of us because, while there are surely consequences, they are never as clear or immediate as in other circumstances.

Technique to Avoid Blaming Your Partner

When your emotional temperature is rising, but you would like to keep it in check in order to continue the conversation, a useful technique involves wearing a thick rubber band around your wrist. As soon as you sense that the heat is rising, snap the rubber band hard enough to feel a sting (but not enough to raise a welt). After that, take a deep breath, exhale slowly and repeat something like the following to yourself: I'm very upset and don't know if I can continue talking without hurting the relationship.

At that point, you have two options:

1. Continue the conversation if you feel sufficiently composed; or

2. Say the code word to your partner, which indicates that you need a break from the conversation to get a hold of yourself.

PRACTICING HOW TO EXPRESS NEEDS WITHOUT BLAMING YOUR PARTNER

Life would be wonderful if you could simply tell your partner, in a caring and respectful manner, how you feel or why you are hurt. Because emotions often get the better of us, it is necessary to figure out <u>what</u> you want to say and practice <u>how</u> to say it before you address your partner. Try the following:

1. Write down what you want to say without editing or analyzing it.

2. Read and edit what you wrote 30 minutes later or when you feel calmer, making sure that it complies with the rules in this book

3. Read it out loud until you are satisfied with the way it sounds.

4. Ask yourself this question: If my partner were upset with me, would I want to be told in this manner. If so, you are done; if not, edit it again and repeat steps 2 and 3.

CHAPTER 3

KEEP BOTH FEET IN THE RING

PREMISE

While it is natural from time to time to feel that a relationship is not working, comments that are dismissive of the relationship may not be made by either partner. Couples can discuss problems only when both parties feel secure in their commitment to each other. If the viability or durability of a relationship is continually called into question, problems between partners can never be effectively addressed.

WHAT YOU SHOULD NEVER SAY TO YOUR PARTNER

Regardless of the level of crisis or the dissatisfaction you feel with your partner, you may not say anything that questions the continuity of the relationship, examples of which are:

I'm sick of this relationship.

We're just not right for each other.

Maybe we should spend some time apart.

We should see each other less.

If you can't change, I'm outta here.

I've had enough of you.

When such statements are made, one partner will use the established code word (asparagus) to stop all conversation and effect a physical separation for 15 minutes.

HOW TO HANDLE YOUR DOUBTS
ABOUT THE RELATIONSHIP

It is natural to be concerned about whether you are with the right person. You may need to give this issue the attention it deserves (confiding in a person you trust or seeing a counselor can prove helpful). In this reflective process, you should give free rein to all your thoughts and feelings, fully exploring your ambivalence about the relationship. Remember that what goes on in your head does not have the ability to hurt your partner, as only actual behaviors can do that. On the other hand, nothing good can come out of a conversation where you discuss with your partner if he is right for you. This type of interaction usually results in making the other feel angry, humiliated or intimidated.

Commonly Asked Question About This Rule: "Since I'm unhappy about many aspects of the relationship and have serious doubts about our future together, how do we continue as a couple?" If someone has fundamental doubts about whether a particular partner is "right" for him, or has emotionally withdrawn from the partner, couples counseling is contraindicated as it may make matters much worse. Individual counseling for each partner is the recommended option for dealing with this sensitive issue. The partner who is ambivalent needs to clarify his thinking, and figure out what course of action makes the most sense; the other partner may need to explore ways of dealing with feelings of rejection, insecurity, or prospective loss.

Most couples who come for counseling still have a commitment to each other, but problems have been shoved under the rug for so long that it threatens the continuity of the relationship. In this case, joint counseling can help a couple identify areas of dissatisfaction and explore ways to effect compromise to revive the relationship.

WHY IS IT HARD TO REFRAIN FROM MAKING DISMISSIVE STATEMENTS?

The person who makes dismissive comments does not necessarily want out of the relationship. If you understand why you are attacking the stability of the relationship, it will be easier to control your impulses. The reasons behind dismissive comments often involve:

Fear that a partner isn't really committed to you. When a partner fears rejection, there is a tendency to try to beat the other to the punch and reject him first. The problem, of course, is that this tends to become a self-fulfilling prophecy.

Difficulty Expressing Yourself. Negative feelings are often suppressed when the skills to express them constructively have not been fully developed. These feelings tend to get bottled up and the pressure inevitably leads to damaging comments about the status or viability of the relationship.

Greater Verbal Ability of a Partner. Rarely are two partners equal in verbal ability. Out of fear of being overwhelmed by the other, the one with the lesser ability often shies away from discussing negative feelings.

There is a real desire to leave the relationship. Let's face it, not all relationships work out. At times, one partner may be in denial about the fragility of the relationship while the other accepts the fact that it is not working out. Talking about this may prove difficult for the partner who wants to break up. He may feel that the other is a "good person" and does not deserve to be hurt, or is simply afraid of what the other's reaction might be. Dismissive comments may then be made with the unconscious desire of provoking the complacent partner into breaking up, thereby shifting the responsibility for this decision.

EXERCISE TO HELP YOU WORK ON YOUR DISMISSIVE TENDENCIES

When a partner has a tendency to make dismissive comments, extensive work is needed to break the pattern. The following is an exercise that can be practiced regularly:

1. When you have dismissive thoughts, write down all the emotions that make you behave this way. Don't edit your thoughts but try to be very specific. Express them, as best you can, in behavioral terms. Here are a few examples:

   I don't like the way he talks to me, he keeps hurting my feelings.

   I can't stand being with such a sloppy person.

   Every exchange turns into an argument. I'm tired of doing this over and over.

   He keeps saying "I am sorry" but refuses to change and I can't stand living this way.

2. Rank them in order of importance with (1) being the least important and (10) the most important.

3. Select the top-three rated items, and write down how you would express them to your partner.

Examine what you have written and, with the rules in this book in mind, edit your items.

4. Read it out loud. See if you like the way it sounds. Think about whether you would like your partner to speak to you in this manner.

Schedule a time with your partner to discuss the most important of the three top-rated items. Do not schedule this discussion when either of you has returned home from work, at bedtime, or when anyone has consumed alcohol or other mind-altering substances. During the discussion, turn off your phones or any other source of distraction.

CHAPTER 4

SAY NO, WITH KINDNESS

"You've got to be more assertive. You can't
just say 'Cock-a-doodle-maybe-do."

PREMISE

A pattern of compliance with a partner's needs based on a fear of saying no usually results in lowered self-esteem and resentment towards the partner. Mastering the art of saying no in a caring way preserves the viability and vibrancy of a relationship,

HOW TO SAY NO WHILE STILL CARING FOR YOUR PARTNER

Here are a number of ways to say no while showing respect for your partner's needs:

Express Discomfort. For people who have trouble saying no, the phrase that works best is: "I'm not comfortable because…" This phrase has the advantage of speaking about one's own feelings, while avoiding the negative characterization of a partner's request or being too vehement about not addressing his needs. After all, it is more difficult to start an argument if all you are doing is describing your comfort level.

Defer Saying Yes or No. When something difficult is asked of us, we can often experience a torrent of thoughts and emotions, which makes it harder to figure out how to respond. In such a case, the best course of action is to delay any exchange until you fully understand the extent of your partner's needs and your feelings about them. The following statements would come in handy, while paying close attention to the tone of your voice:

> I'm not sure how I feel about this…

> I see that this is important to you; so let me give it the full thought it deserves. Can I get back to you later (give a specific time).

> I'm in the middle of doing something right now, can I get back to you later in the day.

Express Your Inability or Reduced Ability. You may not be able to do something because of your skill level, time availability or other commitments. It would be reflected in statements like:

> I'd love to help you out but I don't have available time right now, perhaps I could help you later.

> I'm not the person best qualified to help you out with this, maybe X would be better able to?

Saying No and Yes. This is a way of saying you cannot do something at a specific time or meet the specific need being asked of you, but you are in effect proposing a compromise with statements such as:

I'd love to help you out but can we do it on (date/time).

I'm not exactly comfortable doing it the way you want it, but how about if I help you out in this way?

UNDERSTANDING YOUR DIFFICULTY IN SAYING NO

To improve your ability to say no in a caring way, you need to grasp the types of issues involved in making it difficult to say no to a loved one. Some common difficulties include:

Seeing yourself as a helper or provider. Our definition of being "good" is often confused with being helpful - a pattern that may be reinforced by different cultures and childhood environments.

Fearing conflict. Saying no may generate greater conflict and give rise to other fears, such as your partner being angry or rejecting, or you losing a sense of control.

Needing to see yourself as "nice" or agreeable. It becomes more difficult to say no when you need to maintain a certain self-image or are overly dependent on how other people perceive you.

Fearing disadvantages if you say no. We may fear that if a partner's needs are not met, he may retaliate, making our life more difficult.

UNDERSTANDING REACTIONS TO YOUR PARTNER'S NEED

When you are thinking about how to respond to a need that your partner has expressed, answering the following questions may prove helpful:

> Does complying with this request violate any basic values that I hold?
>
> If it doesn't but I still don't want to do it, what's behind my disinclination?
>
> How much flexibility do I have to meet that need?
>
> Is there something I could offer that might address this request, even partially?

The answer to these questions will guide you in responding to your partner in a loving way, and may help him care about your feelings as well.

SCENARIO

Situation: Calvin and Marlene, a married couple, are raising Chantal, Calvin's teen-age daughter from a previous marriage. They both work but Marlene manages their joint funds and dispenses them based on the family's ongoing needs. Chantal brought home a bad report card and Marlene came down on Calvin, arguing that he is spoiling Chantal by giving her money for no good reason. After engaging in their typical argument –Calvin telling her that she is too uptight, Marlene telling him that he is too indulgent – Calvin caves in and agrees to give money to Chantal only when she does well in school or helps with certain chores around the house. However, when Chantal needs money she plays up to her father who ends up giving it to her, despite none of the conditions being met.

Conflict: In addition to the fact that her stepdaughter is getting money she doesn't deserve, Marlene is even more bothered by Calvin's constant disregard for the agreement they made. She confronted Calvin on numerous occasions to no avail and the tension between them has been more frequent and intense over this issue. Chantal is hearing the arguments between them and starting to take Marlene less seriously and subtly playing them against each other.

Discussion: Calvin finally disclosed that he never really felt comfortable with the agreement he made with his wife. While he generally agreed that his daughter needed to earn some of the money she was being given, he didn't feel that he should be restricted in giving money only based on performance criteria. Yet it was difficult to communicate these thoughts to Marlene, as Calvin was afraid of having to deal with her temper.

Resolution: This was the first time Marlene heard of her husband's disagreement. They finally began to discuss the policy to see how they could revise it in order to accommodate their different views. They eventually agreed that Chantal would get a small allowance each week irrespective of her performance at school or home, but that extra money would have to be earned. Whenever Chantal would come to her father for more money, Calvin would have two choices: he can say no to Chantal if she hadn't earned it; or if it were too difficult to say no, he would suggest that all three of them talk about her request.

CHAPTER 5

YOUR PARTNER WILL NOT COMPLETE YOU

PREMISE

One of the greatest pleasures of a relationship is being able to count on a partner. However, relationship problems occur when one partner becomes overly dependent on the other, needing the partner to act in a way that makes him feel better about himself. No relationship can meet all our needs, so it is important to distinguish between the needs that are achievable as individuals and the ones that are the legitimate province of the relationship. As counterintuitive as it may sound, "you incomplete me," is a better approach to a healthy relationship.

WHAT MAKES IT DIFFICULT TO BE LESS DEPENDENT ON YOUR PARTNER

The biggest impediment to observing this rule lies in the belief that all of our needs should be met by our partner. This leads to withdrawal or aggressive behavior when the partner is unable to comply. When we are single, it is easy to accept the responsibility for our individual needs. However once we enter into a relationship, our perception of this responsibility often gets compromised. A commonly heard phrase is: If he really loved me, he would (fill in the blank).

As a single person, there is a tremendous amount of control over what we expose ourselves to; we manage to avoid situations or people that make us feel uncomfortable. However, in an intimate relationship, we often experience certain vulnerabilities and sensitivities that would not otherwise get stimulated. This can at times seem overwhelming.

HOW TO DIFFERENTIATE BETWEEN HEALTHY AND UNHEALTHY DEPENDENCY

When you feel that your partner's behavior does not meet your needs, ask yourself the following questions:

1. What is the specific need that my partner is not fulfilling?

2. Is that a need that I can fulfill for myself, without hurting the relationship?

3. Are the reactions I am having disproportionate with the need I believe my partner should be meeting?

4. If my reaction is more intense than the situation warrants, what underlying issues of mine are being triggered?

It can be helpful to explore your past familial, platonic, or romantic relationships in order to understand how a need of yours is being played out. The purpose here is to establish patterns that relate less to your partner than your experience and psychological makeup.

Once you understand your own issues, you may be ready, if it is still relevant, to address your partner regarding the situation at hand. Remember, you can only share your needs with your partner if it can be done without blaming him, bringing up the past, or threatening the stability of the relationship.

CHAPTER 6

ACCEPT YOUR PARTNER'S FLAWS

"We're friends, so she accepts me warts and all."

PREMISE

Your partner is imperfect, and so are you. It is impossible to like every aspect of your partner's personality, or to think you can add or subtract features to meet your needs (like Mr. Potato Head). However, through a deeper understanding of your partner, you may be able to accept him as he is, seeing his personality as an intricate fabric best appreciated than tampered with.

When you accept your partner's flaws, he will feel more appreciated and better able to view your flaws with indulgence. This does not mean that partners, out of consideration for each other, will not work to adjust their less attractive traits. It does mean however that the acceptance of each other's flaws will serve to strengthen the relationship.

HOW CAN I FULLY ACCEPT MY PARTNER'S FLAWS?

While it is not easy to accept anyone's flaws, the following exercise may prove helpful. Take two pieces of paper and on one of them, draw three columns.

1. In column one, list all <u>your</u> irritating traits.

2. In column two, on a scale of 1 to 10, rate how much you think this trait irritates your partner (1 is not at all, 10 is tremendously).

3. In column three, record the level to which you think your partner accepts these traits (again on a 1 to 10 scale).

On the second piece of paper, do the same for your partner's irritating traits. Then compare the two lists to compare the degree of acceptance between you and your partner.

If you are less accepting of your partner's irritating traits, you may need to start thinking about how these traits are connected to the ones that attracted you in the first place; what benefits, if any, you derive from these particular traits; and how you can work with these irritating traits to the benefit of the relationship. Bear in mind that whenever you are discussing your partner's irritating traits, you must be prepared to hear similar thoughts from him.

WHAT MAKES IT DIFFICULT TO ACCEPT YOUR PARTNER'S "FLAWS?"

There is a general belief that if a partner cares enough, he will change his problematic traits. This belief can lead to the assumption that irritating behaviors are intentionally inflicted, or that they are a sign of lack of love. As a result, rather than just disliking a trait, we begin to feel angry at the person for having it. This, in turn, leads us to treat our partner as an object of frustration, rather than as a person who, for various reasons, has developed traits we do not like. The more accepting partners become of each other's flaws, the closer they will feel to each other.

CHAPTER 7

HONESTY IS NOT THE BEST POLICY

"Frankly... everything makes your butt look big."

PREMISE

In a committed relationship, we are often driven by a wealth of complex thoughts and emotions. While being honest is generally preferable, we must restrain our expression when it has the possibility of damaging the relationship. "Partner, do no harm," at the very least, should be the principle guiding our communication. While "love has a nasty habit of disappearing overnight" (Beatles lyric) is not literally true, it does symbolize the fragility of the deepest feeling we can have for another. Saying anything that comes into our head under the guise of honesty is not a risk worth taking.

HOW THIS RULE WORKS

You may communicate any thoughts or feelings in a totally honest way to your partner only when what you are saying is <u>caring</u> and <u>respectful</u>. Otherwise, you may not say it.

While this practice may seem to inhibit communication, it does not mean that your feelings should be ignored. By exploring the full range of your thoughts, you diminish their power to drive your behavior. The harder you fight to banish your thoughts from conscious awareness, the more overwhelming they become and the more they fight to be expressed.

If the desire to be honest and say hurtful things to your partner is very strong, use the code word, broccoli, to indicate that you are on the verge of losing it and therefore must quarantine yourself for 15 minutes. If you see that your honest expression continually hurts the relationship and wish to break the pattern, it might make sense to look into past experiences to understand what your partner's behavior may be triggering in you on a deeper level. This is an area where working with a therapist may prove helpful.

SCENARIO

Situation: Lisa and Scott had an unresolved argument before going to bed. Lisa wakes up the next morning, looks over at him and thinks: What an ugly dude, how did I ever wind up with this guy? She is filled with animosity and wants to give it to him. Yet, thinking that a good person would not have these feelings, and taken aback by her level of negativity, she says nothing to him.

Lisa's Reflection: Lisa thought about why she was so angry about last night's conversation. She imagined that she may have felt hurt when Scott spoke to her in a loud and somewhat abrasive voice. This reminded her of other instances in her life when she felt mistreated and disrespected.

Lisa's Action: Later in the day, Lisa, feeling calm enough, said the following to Scott:

> You know, I was thinking about what happened last night because I woke up this morning really feeling upset. I realized that when you raised your voice, it became very hard to continue the conversation. I would hope in the future, even when you are upset with me, that you will try to talk to me a bit more softly.

Analysis: A good decision was initially made by Lisa to say nothing because any expression would have undoubtedly led to an ugly exchange. Lisa's anger, though great, had no power to hurt Scott unless it was expressed, at which time it would become a behavior. By not being honest in this scenario, Lisa bought time to process her feelings without hurting the relationship. Scott was able to take in what Lisa was saying because she spoke from a calm (non-attacking) place. Lisa, in turn, could listen to Scott's explanation about what was going on with him at the time (he was tense about a big meeting coming up at work the next day). This ended up being a real interaction between Scott and Lisa, not just a way for Lisa to extract an apology from Scott (apologies don't go very far unless they are based on a real understanding between partners).

Three purposes were served by this interaction: it enabled Lisa to express herself in a timely manner so resentment didn't fester; it gave Scott a chance to care about how she feels; and it brought them closer because they were able to share and understand what was really going on between them at the time of their argument.

CHAPTER 8

COMPROMISE, COMPROMISE, COMPROMISE!

He wanted a big-screen TV; she didn't.
So they compromised. She let him sit
closer to the screen.

PREMISE

It is absolutely natural for partners to have different needs. However, it is important to understand and accept that our needs will not always be met to our satisfaction. Partners' ability to compromise or find a middle ground between divergent needs, determines the degree of satisfaction and closeness they will experience.

NEEDS THAT ARE SUBJECT TO COMPROMISE

Needs that can be expressed in more concrete, tangible, observable, behavioral, and (even) measurable terms are more likely to be successfully mediated. Examples of understandable needs that would be less effective to start a conversation with include:

> I want to feel more loved.

> I want to feel that you are listening to me when I talk.

> I don't like it when you undermine me in front of the children.

> I would like you to participate more in the upkeep of the house

However, to increase the chances of compromising with your partner you would refine those needs to make them more specific and behavioral, such as:

I would like you to hold my hand when we're out in public.

I would like you to not interrupt me when I talk.

I would like you to avoid telling the children something that contradicts what I'm saying.

I would like you to share the household chores by doing part of the laundry with me.

PREPARATION FOR COMPROMISING WITH YOUR PARTNER

Draw four columns on a piece of paper. In the first column, list the top three needs that you feel are unfilled in the relationship. In the second column, refine those needs to make them as specific and behavioral as possible. In column three, write down specifically what you would say to your partner and say it out loud. In the fourth column, make the appropriate edits so that it complies with the guidelines in this book. Now you are ready to sit down with your partner.

COMPROMISE SCENARIO #1

Situation: Brandon and Elaine have been married for three years. Elaine works for a government agency and gets home around 5:00 PM, and Brandon works for an investment bank and typically doesn't get home till 7:00 PM. While Elaine looks forward to her husband coming home, she experiences disappointment because he always seems "distracted."

Conflict: Elaine would like to interact with Brandon the minute he comes home from work. Brandon would like to decompress a bit after a long day at work and just do his "own thing." They get into arguments because she wants him emotionally available to her, not in his own world. On the other hand, he wants her off his back, feeling that it is selfish to expect him to be "on" the minute he comes home, especially after she has had the luxury of puttering around the house for two hours

Discussion: By listening without interrupting, each partner was able to understand where the other was coming from. Brandon grasped Elaine's discomfort about being unsure when she could talk to him. Elaine could, in turn, empathize with her husband's need to have time to unwind and decompress without having to interact or even listen.

Resolution: Elaine and Brandon agreed on a compromise, which would address their respective needs. When Brandon comes home, he will greet Elaine (by a kiss/hug/etc.). He then has 30 minutes to do whatever he wants without interaction and without any comment from Elaine, after which they can get together to spend their evening in any way they wish.

COMPROMISE SCENARIO #2

Situation: Sherry and Chris have been a couple for a year and a half and recently moved in together. They are now having sex less frequently. This doesn't bother Sherry, but Chris has become dissatisfied and feels "less attracted" to her as a result.

Conflict: Since living together, Sherry and Chris have been bickering more often, mostly over the division of household responsibilities. Sherry likes a place to be relatively neat, with dishes put away after dinner. Chris likes to be spontaneous and not have to put things away right after using them. By bed time, Sherry feels exhausted from her chores and Chris is irritated because things are no longer fun.

Discussion: Chris and Sherry can see that living together has posed unanticipated challenges to their relationship. Each has become resentful of the other over household chores. By openly expressing these feelings, the couple saw the absurdity of this issue undermining their relationship.

Resolution: With a pad, they divided up the household tasks as to who should do what and when. They wound up compromising on the dinner dishes issue: Chris would bus the table, throw away the scraps, and wipe down the table. Sherry would rinse the dishes, put them in the dishwasher, and store the leftovers. They used this process to resolve other household task issues that had caused tension between them.

SITTING DOWN TO COMPROMISE WITH YOUR PARTNER

Here are the guidelines:

1. **Set up a Specific Time to Have a Discussion.** When partners know that there is a specific time to discuss issues, there tends to be less tension.

2. **Set an Alarm to Limit the Time.** There is often a fear that once a discussion starts, it will never end. Considering the different tolerance people have for emotional discussions, it is important to limit the length of the conversation (e.g., to 30 minutes).

3. **One Partner Will Explain His Specific Need.** This means only one need (behavioral in nature), not a laundry list of grievances. At this stage, one

partner just listens to what the other has to say (no interruptions or counter-arguments).

4. **Have a conversation about the specific need**. This stage is where you and your partner begin discussing your need. Just because you have articulated your need does not mean your partner has to agree to meet it. You and your partner will go back and forth, searching for that elusive middle ground.

5. **Write down the compromise and sign it.** This eliminates all possible misunderstanding and heightens the importance of the agreement.

6. **Discussion of the Other's Need**. Repeat the above process discussing the other partner's need.

While having this discussion, eye contact must be maintained. This means real eye contact, not just looking in the direction of the other. When we look into another's eyes, we see him more as a person, not just as an object of frustration. Eye contact makes it harder to retreat into ourselves and it helps us stay in real contact with our partner.

WHAT MAKES COMPROMISING DIFFICULT

While we compromise all the time at work or in our social lives, it often seems more difficult to do so with a partner. Certain beliefs may be interfering with your ability to compromise in an intimate relationship. Here are a few:

The belief that a partner will only agree to things being done his way. It is important to avoid making assumptions, lest they become self-fulfilling. Give your partner the benefit of the doubt.

Compromise is a zero-sum game. There is often a perception that the nature of compromise is that one person has to be compliant with another's need so that the other will return the favor. Keep in mind that a good compromise is when no one accedes to the other's need just because it seems easier or generates less conflict.

One partner feels the other's needs are not appropriate. This often results in one partner undermining the legitimacy of the other's needs by characterizing them as abnormal or neurotic or concluding that they stem from dysfunctional prior relationships.

Feeling less empowered in the relationship. One partner may feel weaker in the relationship because of economic status, emotional dependency, lack of self-confidence or lesser verbal ability.

CHAPTER 9

LISTEN WITHOUT AGENDA

Premise

We all know when someone is truly hearing what we are saying and not just putting in their time listening. We must therefore give our partner undivided attention while he is speaking. When we are able to listen on a deeper level, our partner will feel more cared for and connected to us.

How to Listen More Fully

You can encourage your partner to share more of his thoughts and feelings, as well as to listen and hear on a deeper level by using the following techniques:

Acknowledging: Recognize what the speaker is saying through oral and physical gestures (e.g., uh-uh, "I see," "go on," moving head up and down).

Eye Contact: Look into your partner's eyes, not just in his direction. Note that it is easier for a listener to maintain eye contact than it is for the speaker.

Clarifying: Show interest by asking questions to enhance your understanding.

Paraphrasing: "So what you're saying…"

Summarizing: Make statements that connect the dots of what your partner is saying to reflect your level of understanding.

Body language: Remain in an open physical position by facing the speaker, while avoiding positions that denote boredom or defensiveness; e.g., arms folded across your chest or supporting your head with your hands.

Tuning into the emotions of your partner: Your partner may be experiencing emotions far beyond what he is saying. Demonstrate your understanding without psychoanalyzing. Use simple sentences in your communication, such as "you seem sad while talking about (fill in the blank); or "you're saying 'I'm okay' but I see that you look tearful."

WHAT GETS IN THE WAY OF DEEPER LISTENING

Distractions: Texts, emails, answering the phone, watching TV or just thinking about something else.

Giving advice: Unless specifically requested, avoid telling your partner how to solve the problem or giving him answers you think he wants to hear.

Criticizing: While you may feel critical of what is being said, expressing it may inhibit your partner's ability to be more open with you.

Interrupting: No matter how irresistible the urge may be, cutting off your partner will not encourage him to share more, especially on particularly sensitive issues.

Pressure to Respond: It is not always necessary to respond to everything your partner is saying. It may, in fact, be better to say nothing in some cases. Often, just maintaining eye contact and fully taking in what your partner is saying may be sufficient.

Abrupt Changes in Topic: Switching the conversational subject the millisecond your partner has stopped speaking sends the wrong message. This usually happens when a partner is having an emotional reaction to what is being said and can't wait to answer, or when one is thinking about an answer while the partner is still speaking.

WHAT MAKES IT SO CHALLENGING TO LISTEN MORE FULLY?

In a session many years ago, a client stopped what she was saying, looked at the therapist and said, "You know, you really listen well." This statement touches on how good it feels to be fully listened to, and how rare this experience occurs especially in relationships where there is ongoing conflict.

Because relationships are often marked by resentments, grudges, irritations, time constraints, competing agendas, our ability to listen more attentively is often compromised. The challenge is not simply to rid ourselves of these distractions, but rather to gently set them aside in order to take in what our partner is trying to express.

A major barrier to listening more deeply is the belief that we have to solve our partner's problem and that we are responsible for relieving his distress. This pressure leads us to provide answers when, in fact, our partner may just want to be understood. Deeper listening means keying in to the needs of our partner rather than dealing with your own sense of discomfort.

LISTENING EXERCISE FOR PARTNERS: THE 5 AND 5

This is an exercise that can be used at any time, especially after you and your partner reconvene after one of the code words has been used. Here is how it works:

1. Sit down with your partner and set up an alarm for 5 minutes.

2. One partner explains what is upsetting him, all the while observing the rules in this book.

3. While he is speaking, the other may not talk or make negative gestures of any kind (e.g., rolling one's eyes, smirking). Eye contact must be maintained for the entire five minutes.

4. When the alarm rings, it is reset for five minutes and the person who was listening now has five minutes to talk.

5. When the alarm rings again, you separate for 15 minutes, getting out of each other's line of vision.

LISTENING AND INTERACTION EXERCISE:
THE 5, 5 AND 5

Same as the above exercise, except that you add a third segment of five minutes, during which you will have a conversation about the subjects talked about during your respective five minutes. After the alarm rings again, you separate for 15 minutes. If things go well during this period of interaction, feel free to extend it longer in the future (15-30 minutes is ideal, no longer).

CHAPTER 10

AVOID CLOSE RELATIONSHIPS
WITH THE OPPOSITE SEX

© Mike Baldwin / Cornered

PREMISE

If a relationship of any depth is to succeed, partners need to be emotionally faithful to each other. This faithfulness is often tested when close bonds develop between members of the opposite sex. When there are relationship stresses, a partner may turn to cross-gender friends for sympathy and understanding. These "friendships" feel easier and less fraught with the tension of one's primary relationship. As a result, deeper and often sexual feelings may develop and threaten the stability of the partnership.

HOW DO YOU KNOW IF YOUR OPPOSITE-SEX FRIENDSHIP IS TOO CLOSE?

If any of the following statements is true, your relationship with a member of the opposite sex (or same sex for gay, lesbian and transgender relationships) is TOO close:

You often compare your partner unfavorably to your opposite sex friend (OSF).

You share more of your emotions with the OSF than with your partner.

You appreciate your partner less or feel more negatively towards him after being with the OSF.

You look forward to spending more time with your OSF than with your partner.

You would have less fun if your partner were to join you and your OSF.

To simplify further, let's just say that your relationship with the OSF is too close if your partner, as the proverbial fly on the wall, would NOT feel comfortable with everything that transpires between the two of you.

WHAT MAKES OPPOSITE-SEX RELATIONSHIPS SO ATTRACTIVE?

A committed relationship can feel more transactional, often mired in the daily grind, with partners feeling less emotionally attended to. This may be due to the number of years in the relationship, dual career stresses, child/elder care responsibilities, or different recreational interests. As a result, it may seem attractive to have an OSF where there is no agenda other than to listen and respond to each other; or to share common experiences (like work); or to provide a shoulder for your OSF to cry on or vice versa. Who can deny that it feels good to be appreciated just for who you are? It is especially difficult when your OSF is single and is attracted to you or you to him.

HOW CAN I AVOID HAVING A RELATIONSHIP WITH THE OPPOSITE-SEX THAT IS TOO CLOSE?

There is one cardinal rule: <u>never</u> share any negative information with an OSF about your relationship with your partner. Do not under any circumstances say anything to your OSF that you would not say in the presence of your partner.

It would be helpful to cultivate more same-sex friendships. Through these friendships, we can address needs that our partner may not be able to fulfill and, as a result, strengthen the primary relationship.

At Work: To play it safe, maintain a rapport with the opposite sex that is as professional as possible. If you feel particularly drawn to someone, don't spend time alone with him. If you have to go to lunch with such a person, invite someone else to attend. If that is not possible or practical make sure the conversation adheres to the guidelines in this chapter.

In Social Gatherings: If you had friends of the opposite sex before meeting your partner, you may need to discuss the nature of those friendships with him. In some cases, it may be necessary to modify these relationships or adroitly move away from them. Bring your partner to social events whenever possible.

It is important to note that certain opposite sex friendships may have evolved to a state of (rare) kinship, like a family member. If that's the case, the guidelines expressed in this chapter may be irrelevant for all concerned parties.

MARGARETH'S CONCLUSION

Everyone aspires to be happy, or more precisely to remain happy. But no one is responsible for anyone else's happiness, as the source of one's happiness resides within.

We choose a mate with the hope of experiencing a deeper level of communion. Paradoxically, this remains out of reach when one's ultimate desire is to receive.

The problem is that you may be a taker, which means you always need someone or something to be happy. You can never be satisfied or make someone happy. You deplete your partner to the point of rendering him numb.

Love is the art of giving of oneself. In love as in everything else, one must concentrate on the giving rather than the taking. This in turn creates a bond of love that no adversity can break.

Open your heart and give without expecting anything in return. Give only with the desire to keep your partner happy.

On the other hand, you might be wondering about your fate if your partner is a taker. Well, I'm sure you know by now that it was no accident that you picked him. If you are able to detect that he is a taker, you may be ready for a deeper introspection. If you find yourself constantly complaining about what your partner is not doing or giving, you might be a taker. Stop. Give of yourself. Give only with the hope of keeping your partner's flame ignited.

ABOUT THE AUTHORS

Michael Sands has been a psychotherapist in private practice in Manhattan since 1990, conducting goal-oriented treatment with culturally diverse individuals and couples. His approach with couples has centered on establishing clear-cut rules of communication, mediating the different needs and conflicts that naturally arise in a committed relationship, and examining the underlying beliefs that interfere with this process. A focus of his work has involved occupational issues, including executive coaching, career transitions, job search, and workplace conflict. He has consulted with corporations and non-profit organizations on structuring effective responses to critical incidents and going on site to help affected employees deal with their reactions. He has conducted workshops on a wide range of subjects including stress management, communication skills, conflict resolution, parenting, and goal achievement. He holds a J.D from Brooklyn Law School, and MBA and MS in Social Work degrees from Columbia University. He is a New York State Licensed Clinical Social Worker (LCSW-R). Mr. Sands invites questions, concerns, or feedback at TheRelatonshipZone.com.

Margareth Garnier has been an investigator, lawyer, judge, and administrative hearing officer for the last two decades. As a judge in Haiti, she presided over civil and criminal cases. As a consultant for the US Department of Justice, she assisted in formulating and implementing strategies and rules for overall reform of the Haitian judicial system. For the past ten years, she has been working as a Hearing Officer/Administrative Law Judge, adjudicating suspension cases brought against students in the New York City public schools by the Superintendent. She has been a radio and TV co-host on Haitian affairs and has published several articles on SelfGrowth.com. Ms. Garnier has a Master of Laws (LL.M) from George Washington University and a law degree from Faculte de Droit et des Sciences Economiques in Haiti. She is a member of the State Bar of New York. Ms. Garnier also practices yoga and meditation and has been exploring alternative health medicine for the past four decades. As a life coach, she has helped others discover how to restore their ailing physical and emotional health. Ms. Garnier welcomes inquiries and feedback at TheRelationshipZone.com.

MIKE & MARGARETH, SEPTEMBER 2012

30036100R00046

Made in the USA
Lexington, KY
16 February 2014